Advance praise for *Forever Remembered*

There are so many people who need this excellent book. It is a book about faith and hope and strength and the promise of so much more while never minimizing the depths of the grief being experienced.

—Heather W. Allen, PhD, experimental psychologist/human
factors engineer, SADI Solutions

I have suffered many losses in my life, including the death of our baby at birth and our oldest child as a teenager. With that I also had lost my father by suicide when I was only a teen. I found in Shirley's book comfort from God's Word and a resource to help me understand the stages of grief. I highly recommend this book.

—Linda K. Case, accountant and business owner

Forever Remembered

WHEN YOUR BABY IS IN HEAVEN

SHIRLEY BULEN, RN

WESTBOW
PRESS®
A DIVISION OF THOMAS NELSON
& ZONDERVAN

WestBow Press books may be ordered through booksellers or by contacting:

WestBow Press
A Division of Thomas Nelson & Zondervan
1663 Liberty Drive
Bloomington, IN 47403
www.westbowpress.com
1 (866) 928-1240

ISBN: 978-1-5127-7115-2 (sc)
ISBN: 978-1-5127-7116-9 (e)

Library of Congress Control Number: 2017900314

Print information available on the last page.

WestBow Press rev. date: 01/31/2017

Dedicated to the tiny babies and beloved children who touched our lives so profoundly and so briefly, forever leaving footprints on our hearts, and to the parents of the Wings of Hope support group

Wings of Hope...

Because every life matters

I will not forget you!
See, I have engraved you on the palms of my hands;
—Isaiah 49:15–16

Contents

Acknowledgments ix

Introduction xi

Called to Care 1

The Whirlwind of Grief 5

Comfort of Compassion 21

Comfort of Strength 35

Comfort of Assurance 49

Comfort of Presence 71

Comfort of Heaven 87

Helpful Resources for Baby Bereavement 91

About the Author 93

Acknowledgments

❖ Firstly to our faithful God who chose me and led me on this journey.

❖ My dad, who long ago gave me the incentive for this book, and my mother, who guided me with her compassionate heart.

❖ My children and all of my grandchildren. They have taught me everything I know about parental love.

❖ My husband, Dave, who supported me as I spent hours upon hours listening and writing.

❖ The many parents I have cared for over the years who have shared their sorrows, their hopes, their dreams, and their stories with me.

❖ Crystal and Steve Spire, Renee and Jim Kesterson, and the continuing leadership team of Wings of Hope support group.

❖ Karen Inman, who encouraged and supported me to see this accomplished.

Introduction

As a Registered Nurse, I have attended many couples experiencing the death of their beloved child, either in the womb or during or sometimes after birth.

I have witnessed and shared in the intense grief. We have a God who knows the number of hairs on our heads, calls the stars by name, and is aware of each sparrow that falls from the sky. This same God is also there in each individual experience of grief and pain.

God's compassion moved me to start a support group for the grieving families, aiming to touch lives with His healing, compassionate love.

In this book you will find a compilation of scriptures, poems, notes, and quotes taken from the Heart to Heart support group newsletter I have written over the years. The words of others may help communicate intense feelings of grief and loss and help us realize that we are not alone on this journey.

I hope and pray that as you are read this book you will also realize God's love. If you have experienced a devastating loss, I pray you will find understanding and encouragement for your life's journey. Blessings, Shirley Bulen RN

> You, LORD, hear the desire of the afflicted; you encourage them, and you listen to their cry.
>
> —Psalm 10:17

Called to Care

He has sent me to bind up the brokenhearted, … to comfort all who mourn.

—Isaiah 61:1–2

I began my nursing career in 1970 in the nursery of a local Kansas City hospital. My first day on the unit as a brand-new nurse was very busy. One of our babies was being sustained on a ventilator in the small isolation nursery. We were awaiting the decision to turn off the ventilator. As it turned out, God made the final decision. It fell to me to carry out his after-death care.

In those days families were not encouraged to see or hold babies after they had died. It wasn't offered, and no one asked. The prevailing attitude was "Don't see the baby—just go home, pretend it never happened, and have another baby."

As I carefully bathed his tiny, lifeless body, I thought about his very short life. He had returned to God without even knowing a loving touch. As I bathed him alone in the isolation room, I quietly sang to him, *"Jesus loves me this I know°…"* I carefully dried his fragile skin and wrapped him not in a soft blanket but in a white shroud. *"Little ones to Him belong."*

Covering him with a soft blanket, I held him close in my arms and carried him to the morgue. *"We are weak but He is strong."*

A few months later, a premature baby was stillborn. This mother asked to see her baby. The nurses refused. No one would take her baby to her. They didn't think it was emotionally healthy.

I spoke up. "If she is asking to see the baby she probably *needs* to."

The response came back, "If *you* think she needs to see her baby then *you* take the baby to her."

At twenty years old, I was the youngest, newest nurse on the unit. I took their challenge because it was the right thing to do!

I wrapped the tiny baby girl in a blanket and carried her to her mother. We cried together as we studied her tiny fingers, her toes, and her tiny face. The mother pronounced a name on her and thanked me for the only thirty minutes she would ever have to hold her baby.

God had called me to be a nurse, and now God called me to meet a need: the needs of mothers, families, and nurses who didn't understand the value of those precious moments.

Statistically, 10 to 15 percent of all pregnancies end in miscarriage. Another 1 percent result in loss before or at birth.

As you know, the grief experienced by this particular group of women is very real and very deep. The plans and dreams of a lifetime are shattered.

Losing a child is one of life's most devastating events. It can shake the very foundation of your belief system. It shakes your faith and it rocks families and marriages. Shock, denial, blame, anger, and guilt are emotions that can wreck your life. I liken this to a whirlwind. It comes on suddenly and knocks you clear off your feet. You feel suddenly lost in a dark tunnel of twisting, churning, emotional turmoil.

"Why, God, why?" It's almost a universal question. Does a God of love take away your precious child? In the whirlwind of grief it is easy to lose sight of God and your trust in Him.

I would remind you of two things. In the John 10:10 it says, "The thief comes to steal, kill, and destroy. But I (Jesus) have come that they might have life and have it to the full." It is not God who steals life from us. In Isaiah 43:2–5, we are told, "God is there to give you comfort." God is our comfort! He will sustain you! We may never have the answers we desire, but what we need is the sense that God is there with us during the dark days we do not understand.

The Whirlwind
of
Grief

A voice is heard in Ramah, weeping and great mourning, Rachel weeping for her children and refusing to be comforted, because they are no more.

—Matthew 2:18

It Is I

Pat Schwiebert

It is I whose kicks you will always remember;
I who gave you heartburn that a dragon would envy;
I who couldn't seem to tell time and got your
days and nights mixed up.
It is I who acknowledged your craving for peach ice cream
by knocking the cold bowl off your belly.
I who went shopping and helped you pick out
the perfect teddy bear for me.
I who liked to be cradled in your belly
and rocked off to dreamy slumber by the fire.
It is I who never had a doubt about your love.
It is I who was able to put a lifetime of joy into an instant.

Crystal and Steve's Story

Crystal and Steve were expecting their first baby any day when the contractions started. Wanting to be sure that it really was labor before going to the hospital, they decided to lie down and rest to see if the contractions continued. Crystal was on her left side and Steve next to her with arms wrapped around her as if to comfort and protect. They timed each contraction and practiced the focused breathing they had learned in childbirth class. Between contractions they shared their dreams for life as a family. They were excited, happy, and little apprehensive about the unknown of the coming labor. The contractions continued and indeed were getting stronger.

Suddenly, the water broke. But just as suddenly the gush of water turned to a gush of blood. Their eyes met with fear. Without speaking they knew something was wrong, terribly wrong, but they didn't know what. Steve grabbed the phone and called the hospital birth place.

After getting her name and her doctor's name, the nurse responded with firmness. "Get here as fast as you can."

Steve did not miss the urgency in her voice. They lived only a short distance from the hospital. Silent fear gripped them as they drove. Both knowing…and yet hoping.

Meanwhile at the birth place nurses flew into action, preparing for an emergency. They contacted Crystal's doctor. He left for the hospital in such a hurry that he was followed by a police car all the way. Anesthesia was notified and was there waiting her arrival. The NICU nurses were notified, and they prepared for possible resuscitation of a critical infant.

Steve and Crystal arrived at the birth place and were quickly ushered to a room. The nurses worked in unison as a well-rehearsed team.

As the fetal monitor was placed there were no heart tones heard. Dr. Kent entered the room pushing the ultrasound machine. Sitting on the side of the bed he scanned the abdomen, focusing on the four-chambered heart. Instead of the reassuring steady cadence of the heart fluttering on the screen, the four chambers were still…*completely* still.

After staring at the screen for a long time, he calmly spoke. "There is no heartbeat. I'm so sorry."

The world stood still. Crystal and Steve held each other, crying and stunned.

After assessing that Crystal was not in immediate danger herself, the staff left them alone to grieve and try to assimilate the sudden shock.

They made the necessary phone calls to parents. Steve's parents lived nearby and were quickly on their way. Crystal's parents were in Louisiana. While on the phone long distance with her parents, the door to her room opened and the admission clerk entered.

"I need you to fill out these papers," she stated.

Crystal, distraught and crying, ignored the clerk and continued talking with her parents on the phone. The clerk interrupted again.

"I need to finish this paperwork, or we can't help you," she demanded.

Crystal turned to her and through her tears shouted, "My baby just died! You can't help me anyway!"

Steve's mom escorted the clerk from the room.

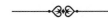

Renee and Jim's Story

Renee and Jim were expecting their first child together. Jim had two sons, Tyler and Cooper, from a previous marriage. They were all looking forward with eager anticipation to the arrival of their little girl.

Renee went to the doctor for her routine seven-month checkup. On this day as she stepped on the scale they noted that she had lost seven pounds. Renee was a little concerned, knowing that she should be having a steady weight gain as the baby was growing. The nurse led her into the exam room for the routine vital signs and measurements. The fetal Doppler was placed in her abdomen to assess the baby's heart rate. The nurse searched in different areas but was unable to find the heartbeat.

"These little ones are sometimes so hard to find," she quipped. "It's like they want to hide from us." After a few more searches, she gave up. "I'll find someone else to try," she stated.

Renee was left in the silent room with only the sound of her own heart beating in her ears.

Soon two nurses entered the room. Once again they began the search for the elusive fetal heartbeat. This time they were hearing the rapidly increasing beat of Renee's heart but not a baby heart. No one spoke a word. The silence hung in the air like a shroud. Without a word, the two nurses left, leaving Renee alone once again with her mounting fear. She grabbed for her cell phone and dialed Jim.

"They're having trouble finding the heartbeat," she sobbed.

"I'm on my way!" Jim fairly shouted into the phone.

The nurses returned with Dr. Torres. "We'll look with the ultrasound," he said.

As they scanned her abdomen, he noted the baby's head, arms, hands, legs, and then placed the scanner over the heart. Renee was watching the screen.

"Why isn't the heart moving?" she shouted. "Her heart should be moving! Why isn't it?" Then she screamed out, "No! No! Uh-uh! No!"

Once again Renee grabbed her cell phone and hit the speed-dial to Jim. Sobbing, the only words she could choke out were, "She's gone!"

On the other end of the phone, Jim was driving to the doctor's office with his thirteen-year-old son Tyler sitting in the seat beside him. Driving as fast as he could, Jim felt as if everything was going in slow motion. Tyler sensed something was seriously wrong.

"Okay, Dad. It will be okay," he said, trying to reassure and comfort his distraught dad. Then he took the phone and texted Renee, "I love you."

Grief Comes Like a Thief

Grief comes into our lives like a thief. We are shocked, hurt, and even bitter. The intensely personal experience may send us into a tailspin of emotions, completely unexpected, always unwanted.

However, just as a warm spring day can evolve into darkening skies and wind and produce tornadoes that leave tragedy in the aftermath, so too can the pattern of life change as quickly. And just as quickly morning comes, the sun shines again, and we are left with the tornado's devastation. Tragedy is a universal experience. It can strike in a number of ways and in many forms. The season of grief comes to us all in one way or another at some time. One of the deepest forms of grief is that of the loss of a child.

We have a God who knows the number of hairs on our heads, calls the stars by name, and is aware of each sparrow that falls from the sky. This same God is aware of your individual experience of grief and pain. He knows your sense of loss, the emptiness in your heart, and deep, lonely sorrow you feel. We know this by the prophecy in anticipation of Jesus:

> He is despised and rejected by men; a man of sorrows, and acquainted with grief.
>
> —Isaiah 53:3 KJV

Grieving is a process. As a parent you never really get over the loss of your baby. You learn to live again. Your journey in life changes, and it changes you. The experience of your baby's death becomes integrated into your life and who you are.

The journey is a painful process, one filled with disbelief, shock, anger, and guilt. You may have anger at your caregivers, your spouse, or God. You may feel guilty for things real or imagined. You may feel guilty for things beyond your control. These are normal experiences in the grieving process. Allowing yourself to *feel* the pain is an important part of healing. While you don't get over it, there is healing along the journey. Eventually you reach acceptance, and you adapt to your changed life.

Your experience with grief becomes part of the new you. The memory of your baby is always there and holds a meaningful place in your life.

Jesus on His earthly walk was filled with compassion for the needs of people.

Describe some feelings you have experienced: _____

_____

_____

_____

> When Jesus landed and saw a large crowd, he had compassion on them and healed their sick.
>
> —Matthew 14:14

Describe a time you been aware of compassion shown toward you: _____

_____

_____

_____

We can know He understands our pain. He loves and cares for us so deeply. You can reach out to Him now. He has offered us comfort. He has given us words of promise and assurance.

> For I am the LORD your God who takes hold of your right hand and says to you, Do not fear; I will help you.
>
> —Isaiah 41:13

Emotional Stages of Grief

The range of emotions that may be experienced after the loss of a baby are typical, though everyone reacts differently. Even those experiencing loss of an unplanned or unwanted pregnancy have been surprised to admit feelings of grief. Don't be surprised by the feelings that you may have, as each of us is an individual, and there is no right or wrong way to feel.

SHOCK AND DENIAL

This is a very common initial reaction to the news that something has gone wrong. It's your body's defense—you just shut down. This is your body's way of trying to protect you from a painful experience. It will gradually wear off to let you experience your grief as you are ready.

ANGER

This is a very normal emotion at this time, and it can be directed at almost anyone—your doctor, nurse, spouse, friend, yourself, or even God. It's important that you find someone to talk this out with and help you work through it.

SADNESS

There many different levels of sadness, from none to very strong feelings of grief. The intensity of sadness may be affected by your perception of the loss. What did this loss mean to you? How long have you planned this pregnancy? Have you had other losses? What kind of support are you getting? Sadness and depression can last anywhere from six months to two years following the loss, especially if you feel that you are unsupported. There are practical ways to cope and help to heal.

GUILT

It seems that most parents can find some way to blame themselves for what happened. Guilt is a very common emotion. Was it something I did? If only I hadn't thought that, done that, or said that! These feelings need to be shared with a trusted person. If, in fact, you have serious guilt feelings, remember that all things can be taken to God. He is the God full of grace who forgives, a Father who welcomes the prodigal home. Turn to Him. Trust Him. Seek counsel in this area with a trusted pastor or counselor.

> As far as the east is from the west, so far has he removed our transgressions from us.
>
> —Psalm 103:12

The pain of grief is numbing. You become lost in it. When did it start? Has it always been here? Will it ever end?

How would you describe the pain you have been feeling? _____

_____

_____

_____

"No one ever told me that grief felt so like fear. I am not afraid, but the sensation is like being afraid. The same fluttering in the stomach, the same restlessness, the yawning, I keep on swallowing." From *A Grief Observed* by C. S. Lewis

What does your grief feel like? _____

_____

_____

_____

Grief

A valley you didn't choose
A whirlwind of emotions
Uncontrollable tears
Anger
Depression
Exhausting
Helpless
Searching for God
Questioning God
Comforted by God
Changing
Change in relationships
Change in marriages
Change in who we are

What changes has this grief brought to your life?

_____

_____

_____

My Daughter Grace
by Jim Kesterson

Oh, how we miss you, your mother and I.

We think about you always and oftentimes cry,

Yearning to hold you and feeling you move;

Kissing your head, the smell of baby shampoo.

I wouldn't get upset at the sound of your cry;

I would just hold you with love, singing a lullaby.

Your skin is like your mommy's, so pretty and fair,

With big, long curls in your precious blonde hair.

Red popsicle stains all over your face

Just like your mommy when she was your age.

You would giggle and splash and play in the tub

And get us all wet and covered in suds.

You would love the outdoors and not want to come in.

We'd go hunting for bugs, and you would have dirt on your chin.

You could help me in the yard and follow me around

With your little plastic mower that makes a real mower sound.

We would plant you a garden and wait for the day

To pick the prettiest daisies for a Mother's Day bouquet.

Your brothers would love you and protect you from harm.

You would have their sense of humor and also their charm.

You would play baseball with Cooper; he would teach you to catch.

And your biggest brother Tyler could help you with math.

You would be spoiled by grandmas and grandpas and aunts alike,

Helping to make cookies and learning to ride bikes.

We would take trips on the holidays and play games in the car,

And I would never get tired of hearing, "Daddy, how far?"

We will still plant a garden in memory of you,

So fragrant and colorful with yellow, pink, and blue.

And out of that garden, there will come the day,

I will pick the prettiest flowers for a Mother's Day bouquet.

I've become a better man all because of you.
I'm growing stronger with God, and your mother is too.
I can say I know an angel and she's my daughter, Grace.
She's hanging out in heaven, and she's saving my place.
I love you, Gracie. Daddy

For I am the LORD, your God, the Holy One of Israel, your Savior...
Do not be afraid, for I am with you.

—Isaiah 43:3–5

Crystal and Steve: Continued

After twelve long hours of labor, Crystal delivered an eight-pound, seven-ounce baby boy. They will never forget how gently Dr. Kent delivered him, kissed his forehead, and said, "God bless you, little buddy." The compassion and tears of their caretakers touched their hearts with bittersweet memories.

Steve cut the cord, and together they welcomed their baby boy, Hunter, into their waiting arms and their broken hearts … only to say hello and then good-bye. It was a blessed and peaceful moment.

Only after the placenta delivered was Dr. Kent able to determine the cause of Hunter's death. It was a rare and heartbreaking condition known as vasa previa when the fetal blood vessels separate from the protection of the umbilical cord or placental tissue and attach to the amniotic membranes (bag of waters). When the bag of waters breaks it causes the vessels to tear and shred. This causes a sudden and complete hemorrhage of blood and results in the immediate death of the baby.

"Why? Why did this have to happen?" The questioning was ever present as they held and loved their otherwise perfect little baby boy.

Why ... Why ... Why?

Why did this happen to me? How can I go on? Will this ever end? It is too much to bear all at once. The shock and numbness become a protection against the unthinkable in our lives. *Sometimes there are no answers.* It has happened before ... and it will happen again. You are not being singled out or punished. Are you angry at God? Why would a loving God allow this? God accepts even our anger. Talk to Him. Even Jesus felt alone when He said, "My God, my God, why have you forsaken me?" (Matt. 27:46).

Questioning is normal, it is not wrong. However, there may be no ready answers.

What are some of your why questions? _____

_____

_____

_____

Take your questions to God. Then trust Him to see you through the days ahead. He has promised to help us. Can we give Him sovereign place in our lives and trust Him to see us through the trials? He loves us deeply and understands our pain. There may be no answers for you now, but you can trust Him to comfort you. He will help you.

Frozen in Time

Grief can seem to freeze us in time. The ability to cope and heal happens only by facing our feelings. Sometimes it happens little by little. Sometimes it takes a long time. Trying to ignore your feelings and bury grief deep inside merely postpones it, intensifies it, and sometimes transfers it into harmful outlets.

Introductions were being made at the dinner table during a business seminar I attended with my husband.

"I'm a labor and delivery nurse, mother of four," I responded as it came my turn.

Dianne, who was sitting next to me, introduced herself as an insurance agent. She shared that she was the mother of three children.

As we began to eat Dianne said quietly to me, "I actually had four children, but my second baby died at birth."

"I'm so sorry to hear that," I replied. "How long has it been?"

"Twelve years," she answered. "I have only recently begun to think about her again. I tried to put it behind me, stuff it way down inside and go on. Everyone said I would forget°… but I haven't."

"And did you name her?" I asked.

"Her name is Ciera. We've never even spoken it since she was buried."

Tears fell from her cheeks to her napkin as she shared the details of the experience and the feelings she had long buried. Grief had been hidden deep in her heart.

"I don't know why I'm telling you. I thought since you were a labor and delivery nurse maybe you have seen other babies die."

It was then I shared with her my work with bereaved parents. Dianne had a deep-seated need to share her story and mourn the death of a baby she loved and missed. The need to share her story flowed out and with it tears. After so many years her healing finally began.

It's never too late to begin to start to heal. Sharing the story is imperative. Sometimes even a stranger can be the one to help you open us. Sometimes it may be someone close to you that you feel you can trust with the hidden pain. As you share, tears may fall, but they are healing tears. Find that someone.

Comfort
of
Compassion

The Spirit of the Sovereign LORD is on me, because the LORD has anointed me to preach good news to the poor. He has sent me to bind up the brokenhearted, … to comfort all who mourn, and provide for those who grieve in Zion—to bestow on them a crown of beauty instead of ashes, the oil of gladness instead of mourning, and a garment of praise instead of a spirit of despair.

—Isaiah 61:1–3

Renee and Jim Continued

Renee and Jim returned home before going to the hospital. They sat silently, numbly staring at the nursery and supplies prepared for bringing a baby home. Renee wrapped her arms around her belly, hugging and holding on to her baby, and cried. Jim could only think, "What can I do to help her now?"

On arriving at the hospital Jim and Renee walked through the birth center lobby full of happy families celebrating new arrivals. Jim rang the buzzer for admittance.

"Can I help you?" replied a metallic voice from the wall monitor.

"Uh, yes, we're here to deliver our baby … it's stillborn."

It was a long labor—twenty-nine hours. Jim wanted to be strong for Renee. It seemed like a slap in the face to have to go through all the long hours laboring and not have a baby to take home after. If only they could go to sleep and wake up to find it was horrible nightmare. Jim stayed at Renee's side through it all, attentive to her every need.

Finally their baby girl was delivered and placed in Renee's arms. Jim broke down. He sobbed. "Noises were coming out of me I didn't recognize," he says. "Renee became the strong one."

Renee felt comfort to at last see her baby daughter. She examined each part of her body, noting her little pouty lip.

"I know she's OK; she's with God," she said through her tears. They held her for a long time, treasuring the moments and feeling at peace. They gave her the name Grace.

Renee's dad and Jim had never had a close relationship. When the family came in the room after Grace was born, Renee's dad went straight to Jim, embraced him, and held him tightly. The grief was shared between one father and another. Renee was overcome with emotion as she witnessed this first miracle of Grace's life. It marked the crumbling of a wall and a bridge built in a relationship that has continued to grow strong.

Mending the Broken Heart

Wounds leave scars—
> The intensity of the pain will fade.
> You will be forever changed.

Time—
> It takes as much time as it takes.
> There is no required amount of time for healing.

How to start—
> Be honest—do you answer, "I'm fine" when asked "How are you?" When we lie to others, we lie to ourselves.

> Give a truthful and honest answer without asking for advice or help—"I'm having a tough day, but thank you for asking."

> The LORD is close to the brokenhearted and saves those who are crushed in spirit.

—Psalm 34:18

You've heard it all:

> "You're young, you can have another baby."
> "Just go home, forget about this, and start over."
> "At least you didn't know him."
> "Aren't you over it yet?"
> "It must have been God's will"

You can't really expect that people will understand how you feel after having a miscarriage or losing a baby or child. Unless they have experienced it themselves, they cannot comprehend the magnitude of the pain. It can be easy to become angry at their reactions and responses.

Usually people want to be helpful, they just don't know how.

We have a choice. We can become bitter and resentful, or we can choose to help them be more aware of the value of that life.

Be forgiving of others—they want to be kind and often don't know what to say or do. Teach them,

> share with them,
>> forgive them.

The choice must be made individually.

> You cannot make it for another.
>> No one can make it for you.

When you have suffered the greatest grief, the very intensity of mourning will eventually subside and diminish. However, there will forever remain teardrops on your heart.

There will never be a replacement. The emptiness will not be completely filled—it will always be held for the love we cannot relinquish.

Nevertheless, comfort comes as we relinquish ourselves to God and His unfailing love. The emptiness can be filled with the love and peace of God.

> I will not leave you comfortless: I will come to you.

> —John 14:18 (KJV)

President Abraham Lincoln also lost a son and knew the experience of deep grief. He eventually found the comfort and relationship he needed at the cross.

"When I left Springfield, I asked people to pray for me; I was not a Christian. When I buried my son — the severest trial of my life -- I was not a Christian. But when I went to Gettysburg, and saw the graves of thousands of our soldiers, I then and there consecrated myself to Christ."

—Abraham Lincoln

Tears are healing. Relief is gained through the expression of grief.

You have collected all my tears in your bottle. You have recorded each one in your book.

—Psalm 56:8 (NLT)

God has all your tears in His bottle! Yes! He knows each tear you shed. That is how much He cares. Your tears are not wasted. God is merciful. He loves you.

The psalmist David mourned his baby who died.

My soul is in deep anguish. How long, Lord, how long? Turn, LORD, and deliver me; save me because of your unfailing love... I am worn out from my groaning. All night long I flood my bed with weeping and drench my couch with tears.

My eyes grow weak with sorrow;... The LORD has heard my cry for mercy; the LORD accepts my prayer.

—Psalm 6:2-10

I Pray God's comfort will surround you.

The pain of losing your child will gradually subside, but the memory will last forever. Eventually you will come to find a new normal for your life. You will arrive by facing just one day at a time.

Jesus, the Prince of Peace, can create a place of peace in your heart that can become evident in your life.

The fruit of the Spirit is love, joy, peace, forebearance, kindness, goodness, faithfulness, gentleness and self-control.

—Galatians 5:22–23

Peace That Surpasses Understanding

I will face each day with:

Love

    I will cherish the relationships in my life.

Joy

    I will look at events of my life as an opportunity to see
    and know God.

Peace

    I will consider God's love and share it with others.

Patience

    I will lower my expectations of myself and others.

Kindness

    I will be grateful for friends God has placed in my life.

    And I will be a friend to others in this valley.

Goodness

    I will choose to live graciously and respectfully.

Faithfulness

    I will trust in God and live my life for Him.

Gentleness

    I will forgive myself and others.

Self-Control

    I will choose the Word of God as the authority and inspiration of my life.

When sorrow is too much to hold, remember that there is a wide support group. Meeting with others to share can change your perspective and provide the arms of love and understanding that you long for. A listing of some support groups can be found at the end of this book. There are also many online support options. And sometimes simply a trusted friend who is willing to listen can provide the love and support you need.

I love the Lord, for he heard my voice; he heard my cry for mercy. Because he turned his ear to me, I will call on him as long as I live. The cords of death entangled me, the anguish of the grave came upon me; I was overcome by distress and sorrow. Then I called on the name of the Lord: "O Lord, save me!" The Lord is gracious and righteous; our God is full of compassion.

—Psalm 116:1–5

Pain of the heart is more powerful than pain of the body.

An odd by-product of my loss is that I'm aware of being an embarrassment to everyone I meet. At work, at the club, in the street, I see people, as they approach me, trying to make up their minds whether they'll "say something about it" or not. I hate it if they do… and if they don't.

—C. S. Lewis from *A Grief Observed*

The Mention of His Name

Unknown author, from darrellsplayground.com

The mention of my child's name
May bring tears to my eyes,
But it never fails to bring
Music to my ears.

Love must be sincere … mourn with those who mourn.

—Romans 12:9, 15

How Long

How long until I can arise each day
When life's greatest tragedy comes my way?
How can I say good-bye
When all I do is cry?
How long to learn how to live,
How to smile,
how to love,
how to give?
How long, O Lord?

Yes, I will laugh again,
And I will cry.
I will live again,
And I will cry.
I will love again,
And I will cry.
My heart will heal;
The scar will be there still.
Memories I will hold,
Stories will be told,

And still, Lord,
I will trust in you.

Shirley Anne

Shirley Anne died silently in her crib, a tiny newborn baby. She was my grandparents' second child, my mother's sister. The year was 1929. Photographs were not yet part of everyday life. They had nothing to capture a sweet smile or even her existence.

One kind, thoughtful friend contacted a photographer to take one picture of her in death. Only one photograph, but so treasured. It was a photograph of love and pain. It documented that she had lived.

I was seven years old when I first saw the photograph. My grandparents kept it carefully wrapped and put away. Only on occasion did they bring it out and share about her very short life. When the tears appeared in Grandpa's eyes it was always time to put the picture away.

I was only seven years old, but I could see what an impact the loss had made on their lives and what a treasure their memory had become. It was a treasure that existed only in their hearts and a single photograph.

My grandparents have since passed on to a blessed reunion with their beloved baby, and the treasured photograph is carefully kept with my treasured possessions, a reminder of love and loss and the value of a photograph.

Only a Photograph

I only have a photograph.
to recall my moment …
mother and daughter.
All my hopes and dreams of her
and my broken heart
captured in a photograph.
I loved her … and let her go.
Her memory burned into my heart,
and a photograph.
With empty, aching arms
I'm left alone
with only a photograph.

Blessed are they who mourn, for they will be comforted.

—Matthew 5:4

Grief That Ambushes

As you begin to venture out and resume living within your world, Grief may suddenly overtake you at a time when you least expect it.

- A friend or coworker will announce she's pregnant or give birth to a healthy baby.
- You may be shopping and it seems everyone is pregnant or pushing a baby stroller.
- You may go to church only to find out they are holding a baby blessing, and you should have been included with your baby.

Each event brings grief anew. Once again you must grieve and let go. For this reason grief is not on a time schedule. It is a process of letting go—a process that cannot be rushed.

Add your own ambushed moments:

_____

_____

_____

_____

_____

Comfort
of
Strength

I can do all things through Him who strengthens me.

—Philippians 4:13

How Do I Go On?

The death of the baby you have loved so dearly will shake you to your very foundation. Your faith may be shaken to the core when faced with sudden grief. All that you have believed about God may come into question.

Prayer is how we express the feelings to God. The confusion, the anger, the questions … Communicate these to God.

Meditate on His words.

In time you will see His loving care in your life. In time He will speak peace into your heart.

Most Beautiful Pottery

Author Unknown

http://www.angelfire.com/tx2/jbrown

A story is told of an Eastern village, which, through the centuries, was known for its exquisitely beautiful pottery. Especially striking were its urns; high as tables, wide as chairs, they were admired around the globe for their strong form and delicate beauty.

Legend has it that when each urn was apparently finished, there was one final step. The artist broke it and then put it back together with gold filigree. An ordinary urn was then transformed into a priceless work of art. What seemed finished wasn't°.... until it was broken.

So it is with people! Broken by hardships, disappointments and tragedy, they can be either discarded or healed. But when mended by a hand of infinite patience and love, the finished product will be a work of exquisite beauty, a life which could only reach its completeness after it was broken.

You may have been broken, but you are not complete until the pieces are reassembled and bonded with a golden filigree of love.

You are a work of art.

> Where can I go from your Spirit? Where can I flee from your presence? If I go up to the heavens, you are there; if I make my bed in the depths, you are there. If I rise on the wings of the dawn, if I settle on the far side of the sea, even there your hand will guide me; your right hand will hold me fast.
>
> —Psalm 139:7–10

Trusting in God will lessen the emotional turmoil. God knows our hearts, He knows our pain, and He is there. He created and knows the baby you long for, and He is there to carry you through your trials. Reach out and take His hand. Trust in His promise to always be with you.

> So do not fear, for I am with you; do not be dismayed, for I am your God. I will strengthen you and help you; I will uphold you with my righteous right hand.
>
> —Isaiah 41:10

Men Grieve Too:
Know Your Strengths

Society shapes the way we express emotions. The expression of concern may be focused mainly on the mother. Indeed she has a physical connection and physical trauma invested in the experience. However, the man in her life is also shaken on two counts—grief over the death of his child as well as the safety and well-being of the mother.

Men are often inhibited in their expression of grief by fear of perceived weakness. Rather they feel required to portray an image of strength and control.

Comfort and understanding can come from other men who also mourn your loss or who have experienced a similar loss. They can be there for encouragement and understanding. However, the grief work you must do on your own.

Look to those strengths and skills unique to you that have sustained you in the past. For many, physical exercise is a good release for emotional energy.

Take up a new interest or refine a current activity.

Are you athletic?
- Jogging
- Tennis
- Join a gym

Are you good with your hands?
- Gardening
- Woodworking

Are you expressive?
- Write, keep a journal, try poetry
- Learn or renew a musical instrument
- Reach out to others

Volunteer time.
- Hospitals
- Schools
- Church

Use your God-given talents and abilities to move forward on the journey through your grief. Turn your pain into positive action. As you do, you will find yourself moving toward healing.

What areas have you used in the past to conquer stress or grief?

_____

_____

_____

Dealing with Anger

Anger is a very natural part of the grief process. It may be directed at people, at God, or just anything convenient.

Being able to feel and experience anger without becoming consumed by it is challenging.

There is a story of a Native American elder who was telling his grandson about his feelings following a loss. Here is the meaningful conversation:

> "I feel as if I have two wolves fighting within myself. One is hateful and vengeful, the other is loving and compassionate," he told his grandson.
>
> "Which one will win" the grandson asked.
>
> "The one I feed," answered the grandfather.
>
> —Cherokee Legend

God understands and accepts our feelings. Prayer is a place where we can be open and honest about our anger and then leave it behind. God can help us find creative and positive ways to manage the anger.

Handling the Crisis Together

Living through such a crisis together can be devastating to a couple's relationship. Everyone grieves differently.

Generally speaking, women are more likely to express themselves emotionally. It seems easier for women to allow themselves to cry.

Men tend to grieve more silently. They try to be the strong, protective people. He may turn to acts of problem-solving, desiring to be the fix-it person but then find himself frustrated that he cannot fix this one. Men may sometimes bury themselves in work, stuffing down their own grief.

These differences can actually come between a couple and cause conflict if they don't understood what is actually happening.

It is important to give each other the space needed to grieve in your own way. Be careful not to judge each other's grief responses. Maintaining good communication is key.

Remember, you have each experienced the same traumatic episode in your life, but your experience was different and viewed from a different perspective. However, you have also experienced it together in a way that no one else has. It can be a time to draw strength from each other, but try not to place expectations on each other.

Helpful Tips for Couples

❖ Don't assign blame to each other.
❖ Set a time to talk each day and share your feelings.
❖ Lower you expectations of yourself and each other.
❖ Face one day at a time.
❖ Accept each other's way to grieve.
❖ Touch, hold one another.
❖ Find time to laugh together.
❖ Request help when needed from family, friends, or church.
❖ Join a grief support group.
❖ Seek professional counseling.

How are dealing with your grief together? _____

_____

_____

What are your strengths? _____

_____

_____

What are your weaknesses? _____

_____

_____

In what areas might you need help? _____

_____

_____

Overcoming Burdens of Life

Did you know that an eagle knows when a storm is approaching long before it breaks? The eagle will fly to some high spot and wait for the winds to come. When the storm hits, it sets its wings so that the wind will pick it up and lift it above the storm. While the storm rages below, the eagle is soaring above it.

The eagle does not escape the storm. It simply uses the storm to lift itself higher. It rises on the winds that bring the storm. When the storms of life come upon us—and all of us will experience them—we can rise above them by setting our minds and our beliefs toward God. The storms do not have to overcome us. We can allow God's power to lift us above them.

God enables us to ride the winds of the storms that bring sickness, tragedy, failure, and disappointment in our lives. We can soar above the storm. Remember, it is not the burdens of life that weigh us down; it is how we handle them.

> But those who hope in the LORD will renew their strength. They will soar on wings like eagles; they will run and not grow weary, they will walk and not be faint.
>
> —Isaiah 40:31

A Cup Overflowing

Into every person's life comes a cup of suffering. Jesus can relate in this. He was "a man of sorrows, acquainted with grief" (Isa. 53:3 NKJ).

Jesus experienced agony in the garden of Gethsemane. He asked, "My Father, if it is possible, may this cup be taken from me. Yet not as I will, but as you will" Matt. 26:39.

Jesus understands the pain of grief and agony. However, He poured out His lifeblood for the love of His people … for love of *you*. Because of that we have the hope of eternal life with Him. He broke death's hold through His resurrection, giving us hope.

> In my Father's house are many rooms; if it were not so, would I have told you that I am going there to prepare a place for you?
>
> —John 14:2

He has gone ahead of us to give us life and to prepare a place for us. We can live eternally with Him. In that hope of eternal life is also the hope of a great eternal reunion. Halleluiah!

Kelly and Daniel's Story

Kelly and Daniel put off starting a family until their careers were established. But now they were ready and excited to start this new venture of parenting.

The pregnancy was progressing normally. Like all new expectant parents they were learning all they could and enjoyed planning a nursery and shopping for strollers and baby clothes for their much-anticipated little one.

Because Kelly had postponed childbearing until her mid-thirties, a level II ultrasound was ordered at her twenty-week checkup as well as consultation with a perinatologist.

Kelly and Daniel's world began to fall apart. They learned they were having a baby boy, but also the higher quality of the ultrasound indicated there was a problem with the baby's legs. They had the appearance of having been broken and healed many times. Consultation with a genetics counselor followed and more tests. They feared the baby was suffering with a fatal diagnosis.

Because of the severity of the diagnosis, they were given the option to terminate the pregnancy if they desired.

"Oh, no," Kelly responded. "That is not something I will do."

Again she was encouraged to consider termination. "Take some time to think about it," the perinatologist suggested. "You don't have to carry a baby that you know will not survive."

In one day, Kelly and Daniel's dreams came crashing down. So overwhelming was the news that they could hardly comprehend what was being said to them. The word *fatal* swirled around and around, obliterating every other thought.

Kelly called me. We talked about what would happen, knowing the baby was going to die. The baby could die in labor, with best survival being maybe a few hours. In those very few hours, they would have the total of their family time together. There would be many struggles to face until that day as well.

Strangers always feel connected with pregnant women, asking questions such as, "When is your baby due?" or "Do you know if it's a girl or boy?"

A lot of strength would be required to get through the rest of the pregnancy.

Kelly and Daniel sought out the counsel of their pastor. Together they looked into God's Word and prayed for guidance and strength.

Prayer requests went out. People Kelly and Daniel didn't even know contacted them to offer prayer and support across the country and as far away as Canada.

When they returned to see the perinatologist, the test results gave a final diagnosis: a rare and severe skeletal defect that is always fatal.

Once again they were given the option to terminate. Kelly and Daniel were firm in their resolve to allow God to determine the outcome. "We love this baby," they said. "God sent him to us, and we will care for him and love him until he's born. We will celebrate his birth and his life for as long as God gives him to us."

And so it was. Kelly delivered by a scheduled C-section. Family, friends, and three closely involved pastors gathered at the hospital. Daniel lovingly carried his son, Nathaniel, in his arms out of the surgery. Surrounded by love, Nathaniel lived a few short hours and died peacefully with his parents attending him. The funeral held for Nathaniel was a beautiful service of celebration.

Kelley and Daniel have seen the short life of Nathaniel touch many lives.

Grief is deep and overwhelming. But the love shared brings meaning to the suffering. It is a love that is not forgotten, but treasured; a love that is a testament of hope in the eternal wholeness in the presence of the Savior.

Endure

If I can endure for this minute
Whatever is happening to me,
No matter how heavy my heart is,
Or how dark the moment may be.
If I can but keep on believing
What I know in my heart to be true:
That darkness will fade with the morning
And that this will pass away too,
Then nothing in life can defeat me.
For as long as this knowledge remains
I can suffer whatever is happening,
For I know God will break all the chains
that are binding me tight in the darkness
And trying to fill me with fear.
For there is no night without dawning,
And I know that my morning is near.

Weeping may endure for a night, but joy comes in the morning.

—Psalm 30:5 (NKJ)

Comfort
of
Assurance

Whoever drinks the water I give him will never thirst. Indeed the water I give him will become in him a spring of water welling up to eternal life.

—John 4:13

Crystal and Steve Continued

Steve and Crystal kept baby Hunter with them in their room. This was the only time they would have with him. They treasured their time alone with him after the family had gone. They were fearful of what would happen to him when they let him go. They wondered what was the next step. Where would he be?

They were afraid to know the answers, they were afraid to not know, and they were afraid to ask. So they kept him by their bed through most of the night. Soon a nurse reassured them, "I will keep him in the nursery, and you can ask for him to be brought back to you at any time."

With that promise, they let him go to the nursery and they finally slept.

The next day Pastor Baker arrived. He offered to take baby Hunter to the funeral home himself. Gently wrapping Hunter in soft blankets, he held him close in his arms and talked to him as he carried him down the hall and out the door of the birth center. It was a comforting memory of their good-bye.

Crystal continued to wonder why this had happened to them.

Eight months earlier, before she realized she was pregnant, Crystal and her mother had attended a Women of Faith conference. Joni Eareckson Tada was a featured speaker. Joni has been a quadriplegic since the age of sixteen. In sharing her journey, Joni related her own questioning of God. A friend told her, "God doesn't owe you an explanation. He provides you with the comfort and the strength you need."

Crystal's mom reminded Crystal of that statement. It became a turning point for Crystal and Steve. Together they prayed, "It's your plan, God. Comfort me, lead me, show me the good that can come from all of this." God is sovereign; God is still God.

Crystal and Steve have found that in surrendering they have received great strength. God's spirit has been evident in their lives, and they recognize that the blessings from Hunter's life have been multiplied many times over.

Where Is God?

God has promised in His Word never to leave us. He is there with you in the whirlwind°...
and in the valley. You may not see Him, you may not feel His presence, but He is there
keeping watch over you.

There are others who have walked this valley before you. In their experiences you can
find understanding. They know the pain, the anguish, the anger. They can be examples of
courage, faith, and future hope.

Therein is the value of joining a support group. The ability to express feelings no one
seems to understand is so valuable. Seeing that others cope and how they do so is a great
learning experience. Knowing you are not alone is so important as you try to gain a new
stability and a new normal for your life after the devastation of the whirlwind.

Renewal Each Day

At the end of each day review the events of the day. Find at least one incident to be thankful for. Thank God for that. Write it down. Keep a gratitude list.

- a work spoken
- a bird singing
- a flower blooming
- _____
- _____
- _____

When you feel discouraged, look back over your gratitude list and see how God has touched your life. Then you can renew your trust in God for one more day.

You also are God's creation whom He loves. He desires your heart and diligently seeks a loving relationship with you.

> I have loved you with an everlasting love; I have drawn you with unfailing kindness.
>
> —Jeremiah 31:3

Does God Care about My Baby?

Babies and children are very important to God. This is made very clear in scripture. There are many treasures to be found in Psalm 139 that tell how special and loved babies are in God's eyes:

> For you created my inmost being; you knit me together in my mother's womb. I praise you because I am fearfully and wonderfully made; your works are wonderful, I know that full well. My frame was not hidden from you when I was made in the secret place, when I was woven together in the depths of the earth. Your eyes saw my unformed body. All the days ordained for me were written in your book before one of them came to be.
>
> —Psalm 139:13–16

We may not understand what purpose there is in a life so shortly lived. But God has purpose for every person created. God has purpose in the life of a baby even as he is formed in the womb. You may not understand the purpose of your baby's short life, but God's purpose is surely not in the death but in the life.

> Before I formed you in the womb I knew you, before you were born I set you apart.
>
> —Jeremiah 1:5

God knows the destiny and purpose of every baby created. Even when He takes them home to Him, He knows what blessings may reach across time.

God is faithful. God has a sovereign plan and purpose, and it is for our good when we trust in Him.

> "For I know the plans I have for you," declares the Lord, "plans to prosper you and not to harm you, plans to give you hope and a future."
>
> —Jeremiah 29:11

A Message of Hope

I remember my affliction and my wandering, the bitterness and the gall. I well remember them, and my soul is downcast within me. Yet this I call to mind and therefore I have hope: Because of the Lord's great love we are not consumed, for his compassions never fail. They are new every morning; great is your faithfulness. I say to myself, "The Lord is my portion; therefore I will wait for him "The Lord is good to those whose hope is in him, to the one who seeks him; it is good to wait quietly for the salvation of the Lord. It is good for a man to bear the yoke while he is young.

—Lamentations 3:19–27

...we who have fled to take hold of the hope set before us may be greatly encouraged. [19] We have this hope as an anchor for the soul, firm and secure.

—Hebrews 6:18–19

You Are Valued

Our Heavenly Father knows the smallest details of our lives. He counts the stars, and He knows the number of the hairs on our heads. He knows every part of our pain and sorrow.

> Are not five sparrows sold for two pennies? Yet not one of them is forgotten by God. Indeed, the very hairs of your head are all numbered. Don't be afraid; you are worth more than many sparrows.
>
> —Luke 12:6–7

You are infinitely more important than the sparrow. When you feel your life has been devastated by the storms of life it is easy to lose sight of the Lord. Do not let despair take hold. In these moments it is important to trust in God's presence and His sovereignty even when we don't understand. Faith is about walking through the storms and the valleys trusting in the Lord's guidance. He will never leave your side. You can call on Him, and He will sustain you.

> I will never leave you nor forsake you.
>
> —Joshua 1:5

Life is not easy. Not ever. There are many troubles in our lives. You have experienced the worst of troubles. We were not promised things would be easy. Trust Jesus, for He has promised peace and victory, even victory over death. We don't understand it all, but we can trust it.

> I have told you these things, so that in me you may have peace. In this world you will have trouble. But take heart! I have overcome the world.
>
> —John 16:33

Six Steps to Healing and Resolution

1. **Start your day with prayer.** Scripture is a good guide for prayer.

    > "May the God of hope fill you with all joy and peace as you trust in him, so that you may overflow with hope by the power of the Holy Spirit"

    > —Romans 15:13.

    Pray the scripture back to God. For example: "God, please fill me with your joy and peace as I trust in you, so that I may overflow with hope by the power of your Holy Spirit."

2. **Take care of yourself:** Stress is a killer. Be kind to yourself, take a walk, exercise, and so forth.

    What is your best stress reliever ? _____

    _____

3. **Invest yourself in others:** Taking on a cause or need helps you find purpose and helps make your world a better place. Do acts of kindness in honor of your child, such as donating children's books to a school or library, donating to a crisis pregnancy center, or donating to the Make-a-Wish Foundation.

    What cause or activity could you invest in?

    _____

    _____

4. **Cry:** Tears are healing. Tears remove stress toxins from your body. Unshed tears leave a distorted vision of the world around you. Allow yourself to cry.

5. **Laugh:** It is still the best medicine. Sometimes you may laugh and then cry, realizing you have not laughed for a while and maybe feeling guilty for laughing. These are normal thoughts, but laughter will come again. It is healing and necessary.

What did you feel the first time you laughed again?

_____

_____

6. **Practice kindness:** sometimes people just don't know what to say and may say something that sounds offensive when they mean to be helpful. You may feel like snapping back to everyone who speaks to you. Try to respond gracefully. Try these: "Thank you." "Thank you for caring." "I am having a tough day today." or "I love you."

When is it hard to say kind words? _____

_____

_____

Like Silver Refined

As you travel the journey of grief and pain it is important to experience and feel the emotions that confront you. It is part of the healing to allow yourself to vent. Feel your pain. Express it. Find someone to talk to, such as a pastor, friend, counselor, or join a support group. Keep a journal and record your feelings.

If you try to run away, you will only become a bitter person. By working through the many emotional upheavals in the whirlwind of this journey you may become more compassionate, more sensitive, and more supportive; you may find it in yourself to reach out to others who are also experiencing a whirlwind of grief.

Healing doesn't mean forgetting. Healing is the change in you. You will never be the same person you were before. You will come to a new normal, and you will become a new person. The memory and love of the child you lost becomes a part of you and a part of your life. Like silver in the refiner's fire, healing is precious, beautiful, and of great value.

> This third I will bring into the fire; I will refine them like silver and test them like gold. They will call on my name and I will answer them; I will say, "They are my people," and they will say, "The LORD is our God."
>
> —Zechariah 13:9

Renee and Jim Continued

Renee and Jim have seen their lives change completely because of Grace.

Instead of turning to anger, Jim turned to God. For the first time, he opened a Bible and began to read. He read the Psalms, he read Job. Then he reread Job°… five times in two days. He found a counterpart in Job as he read of his suffering and his unfailing trust in God.

It strengthened and comforted Renee to see Jim turn to God as he never had before. Together they found strength in God's presence daily.

"Jim!" He awoke suddenly when he heard someone call his name. But there was no one around, so he went back to sleep.

"Jim!" Again he was awakened.

"Renee, do you need something? I heard you call me."

"No, Jim, I didn't call you," she answered.

The next night it happened again. He questioned Renee again. No, she hadn't called him. Jim shared these strange incidents with a friend.

"It's probably God calling you, Jim. Why don't you try talking to God?"

When it happened a fourth time, "Jim answered, "God, are you calling me? I'm listening. I want to follow you. I want you to be Lord of my life. I don't understand why my daughter Grace had to die, but I will trust you."

Jim had become a new man in Christ.

"You have to admit that you are vulnerable and needy," Jim says. "I have found purpose in my life. This relationship with God is bigger than anything I ever imagined. And it is because of Grace that I am where I am today. God's grace is a gift from my daughter Grace."

Share a time when you have experienced God's grace:

_____

_____

_____

_____

How Long?

The loss of a child is a lifelong grief. Parents do not ever stop grieving. It may vary in intensity, but it will return again and again.

As you go through the seasons of life, grief will assault you anew—a cruel reminder of the scar on your heart. Each time you must work through the feelings once again.

Grief can't be ignored. You can mask it, stuff it, or deny it, but eventually it must be dealt with. Grief is hard work, but it must be done in order for healing to begin.

Each time pain and grief overtake you it is important to acknowledge the pain and allow the healing tears to flow. As you allow yourself to feel the emotion, you can readjust once again to the reality of living with the loss.

After such an acute loss, as mourning begins to subside, there will remain an inconsolable gap. Other experiences come, other love comes, but nothing ever fills that gap. That's as it should be—always a love that should not be relinquished.

In this sad world of ours, sorrow comes to all°...

> It comes with bitterest agony ... Perfect relief is not possible, except with time. You cannot now realize that you will ever feel better ... And yet this is a mistake. You are sure to be happy again. To know this, which is certainly true, will make you become less miserable now. I have experienced enough to know what I say.
>
> —Abraham Lincoln, reflecting on the death of his child.

An Appointed Meeting

Danielle had been devastated by the loss of her first baby. She came to the Walk to Remember and brought her mother-in-law, Sherry. Danielle introduced us, telling me Sherry had also lost her firstborn son.

"Thank you so much for doing this," Sherry said. "I never had a chance to grieve my son. I never even saw him. I was young, and everyone thought that would be best. This event has finally offered me the chance to acknowledge him and put some closure to the grief I have held deep inside for twenty-five years."

"I'm so sorry," I responded. "Would you like to tell me more about it?"

"I was very young," she continued. "He had a malformation that was incompatible with life and only lived about four hours." I was surprised as she gave me a few more details. Then I surprised her.

"I took care of your baby."

It had been twenty-five years earlier at another hospital. I remembered her name and how much her experience had impacted my life and career.

We talked about his brief life. At the time I had offered her the option to see and hold her baby, but the prevailing attitude was that would not be the best thing. Her family had encouraged her to not see the baby. Now I had the opportunity to tell Sherry how I had held her precious baby and how he had passed from life quietly and easily.

Tears flowed down her face as she hugged me. "It's is so good to talk with someone who knew my baby and to hug someone who hugged my baby."

Through her own experience, Sherry was able to offer support and comfort to her daughter-in-law and also find resolution for her own buried grief.

And I was able to see God at work as the caring ministry of perinatal loss support came full circle in my life.

Acceptance

The sun rises every morning. We open our eyes. We breathe. Life goes on. Sometimes a person may feel pressured to get on with it, but we all must remember that each person works through grief at their own individual pace. If we do our grief work, resolution does eventually come. How do you know when it does? There are a few identifiable signs of grief recovery and resolution:

- Accepting the reality of the loss.
- Experiencing the pain of grief.
- Adjusting to daily life without the loved one.
- Reinvesting in others.

Just because we see the signs of acceptance does not mean there will no longer be days of sadness and grief. But the intensity of the grief will gradually lessen.

"We as human beings never 'get over' our grief, but instead become reconciled to it … the sense of loss does not completely disappear, yet softens and the intense pangs of grief become less frequent."

—Alan D. Wolfelt, PhD

Choose

To live again
To face tomorrow
To allow the broken heart to heal

God's Promises

I will never leave you nor forsake you.

—Joshua 1:5

For this God is our God for ever and ever; he will be our guide even to the end.

—Psalm 48:14

Then you will call, and the Lord will answer; you will cry for

help, and he will say: Here am I.

—Isaiah 58:9

Jesus said to her "I am the resurrection and the life. He who believes in me will live, even though he dies; and whoever lives and believes in me will never die. Do you believe this?"

—John 11:25–26

When have you experienced God's promises? _____

_____

_____

_____

God's Purpose

I have come that they may have life, and have it to the full.

—John 10:10

Then they asked him, "What must we do to do the works God requires?" Jesus answered, "The work of God is this: to believe in the one he has sent."

—John 6:28-29

For I know the plans I have for you," declares the Lord, "plans to prosper you and not to harm you, plans to give you hope and a future.

—Jeremiah 29:11

When have you seen His purposes?

_____

_____

_____

God's Precious Love

For God so loved the world that he gave his one and only Son, that whoever believes in him shall not perish but have eternal life.

—John 3:16

keep yourselves in God's love as you wait for the mercy of our Lord Jesus Christ to bring you to eternal life.

—Jude 1:21

We love because he first loved us.

—I John 4:19

When have you experienced His love?

_____

_____

_____

Prayer of Renewal

Father, as I stood at my open door, the sunshine and cool morning air dried the tears on my cheeks. I watched a squirrel make his way down the trunk of a tree, beginning his morning search for food.

Amid the sound of traffic, I am aware of the stillness, the quietness of your world. Birds singing praises to the new day, fresh blades of green grass struggling through the brown of the winter lawn.

I am thankful for these moments of rest that bring hope and peace, and I realize, once again, that you care, that you love, that you know the anguish of my heart, and I am renewed in your grace.

> I lift up my eyes to the hills—where does my help come from? My help comes from the LORD, the Maker of heaven and earth.
>
> —Psalm 121

Seasons of Grief

The summer of grief is bright, hot, and unrelenting like the burning sun, interspersed with periods of respite that allow a brief escape from the new reality.

The fall of grief is gray, crisp, like autumn leaves always crunching beneath our feet no matter how we try to sweep it away. Then tears like rain leaving the world and our soul soggy and mournful.

The winter of grief is cold, frozen in time with shock at the unexpected. We experience anger. Anger at God, at people close to us, at caregivers, and even people we don't know who are pushing strollers or swings at the playground. We internalize anger and sink into depression. We are left cold and alone.

The spring of grief is tearful. Tears fall on us like rain. It may come suddenly in crashing thunderstorms, sometimes giving way to a gentle, steady cleansing. Yes, tears can be cleansing to the soul, leaving space for the bright color of promise, new buds of hope, and the wonderment of restoration.

The seasons change. They ebb and flow, sometimes blending into each other. So is the journey of grief. Life is forever changed, yet through living the seasons of your grief, cleansing, renewal, and resolution are possible.

> To everything there is a season, a time for every purpose under heaven: A time to be born, and a time to die … A time to weep and a time to laugh, a time to mourn and a time to dance …
>
> —Ecclesiastes 3:1–4

Peace in Memories

Hold on to your memories. Embrace the bittersweet memories of love and joy that grew within you and that you now have released to God. In time, embracing the memories can bring peace and joy in your life.

It is better to have loved and lost than to never have loved at all.

—Alfred Lord Tennyson

In quiet moments of prayer comes peace that transcends understanding. God is the very source of all peace. He brings peace into all situations.

The peace of God, which transcends all understanding, will guard your hearts and your minds in Christ Jesus.

—Philippians 4:7

Now may the Lord of peace himself give you peace at all times and in every way. The Lord be with all of you.

—2 Thessalonians 3:16

The deeper that sorrow carves into your being, the more joy you can contain.

—Kahlil Gibran, from *The Prophet*

Share your deepest sorrow: _____

_____

_____

Share your deepest joy: _____

_____

_____

Share your times of peace: _____

_____

_____

Forever Remembered

Life does continue on. And so may love.

In remembrance: your children live through you.

You will always carry in your heart the love for your child. That love will form who you are and who you will become. Because of that, your child's presence will always be with you.

In lives of others: through kindness done in memory of your child. The love expressed in memory of his or her very short life will live on and affect the lives of others.

Your child will not be forgotten,

> Not by you,
> > not by God

I will not forget you! See, I have inscribed you on the palms of my hands.

—Isaiah 49:15–16

Comfort
of
Presence

Here I am! I stand at the door and knock. If anyone hears my voice and opens the door, I will come in and eat with him, and he with me.

—Revelation 3:20

Earlier in chapter one, I discussed who the thief is, the one who is on a mission to destroy us. It is Satan, the devil. He is out to steal, kill, and destroy. Just as a reminder of this, we can look to Peter for advice and help.

> Be alert and of sober mind. Your enemy the devil prowls around like a roaring lion looking for someone to devour. Resist him, standing firm in the faith, because you know that the family of believers throughout the world is undergoing the same kind of sufferings.
>
> —I Peter 5:8-9

There are others suffering in the same place you are. Other babies die, other parents are grieving with broken hearts. There is comfort in the understanding of others.

> And the God of all grace, who called you to his eternal glory in Christ, after you have suffered a little while, will himself restore you and make you strong, firm and steadfast. To him be the power for ever and ever. Amen.
>
> —1 Peter 5:10–11

God has called you to restoration through Jesus. God understands the suffering—His Son Jesus experienced the cross for love of you.

More Steps to Healing

- ✓ Confront the reality. Maintain memories. Recognize the goodness and love you have experienced.

- ✓ Develop a new sense of self that reflects that part of your character. You are still a mother or a father. Be a parent to your memory.

- ✓ Find new ways to function. Meet the daily needs of your existence.

- ✓ Discover new areas of emotional investment.

- ✓ Surrender to God's comfort. Allow faith to move you into reliance on Jesus Christ.

These are difficult steps. The process does not happen easily. They are choices you make each day.

You can once again experience joy. That is not to mean that you will not feel the pain or shed the tears. Grieving is acceptable. Grief may last a lifetime, but you do have choices.

You can remain in despair and use anger and bitterness as the mortar to build a stone wall around you, or you can choose to live by expressing your feelings, opening your heart, and trusting God. Death and grief are a part of life. Your experience of grief can mold you into a mature person of faith and character.

Choices are not easy, but they determine how you will allow circumstances to shape you. God's love for you is not defined by the circumstances in your life, but rather by His suffering on the cross for you.

Joy is not life without pain but rather recognizing the presence of God in our lives. Joy is the peace of His presence.

> … I will turn their mourning into gladness; I will give them comfort and joy instead of sorrow.
>
> —Jeremiah 31:13

> … weeping may stay for the night, but rejoicing comes in the morning.
>
> —Psalm 30:5

Out of the Ashes

Steve and Crystal and Jim and Renee have become close friends and coleaders in the Wings of Hope ministry, a support group and outreach for other parents who have been through the devastating experience of loss.

Is a support group necessary? Support is an important part of growing through grief. It may not be necessary for everyone, but many people find it a safe place to share with others who understand—dad to dad, mom to mom. There may be tears, there may be laughter, and there may be service.

A support group is *not* a place only to cry and stay stuck in grief. A support group is a place to learn how to live again.

You will learn from each other. You will find that you are not alone. There is help and comfort in knowing others who have experienced a similar loss. Do not be afraid to take that initial step.

Celebration of Remembrance

Christmas is the celebration of the birth of Jesus. He is the gift of God's love. The fulfillment of the gift wasn't in His birth but rather in His crucifixion and resurrection.

Following His very powerful time in ministry with the disciples, Jesus instituted with them a new covenant at the Last Supper. They did not know what was coming, but Jesus did.

> And he took bread, gave thanks and broke it, and gave it to them, saying, "This is my body given for you; do this in remembrance of me." In the same way, after the supper he took the cup, saying, "This cup is the new covenant in my blood, which is poured out for you."
>
> —Luke 22:19–21

Jesus poured out His blood out of love for us, and in that is our hope. He tells us to remember°...

Remembering and celebrating brings healing to our souls. Remembering and celebrating the presence of these precious ones in our lives acknowledges the love we received and its value and significance in making us who we are.

Create remembrances for those little ones whose footprints are forever on your heart. Remember the joy

Reflect on the pleasures you experienced during the pregnancy.

Such memories of love you can treasure. It was a precious time, a precious love, and a precious life.

When you lose someone you love, healing comes not in forgetting, but in remembering.

Write your memories of the love you had: _____

_____

_____

_____

_____

_____

Stones of Remembrance

In Joshua chapter four, he was leading the Israelites and bringing the Ark of the Covenant into the land where God had led. They needed to cross the Jordan River, which was flooding. God separated the water for their passage, just as He had the Red Sea.

As they came onto the other side, God instructed Joshua to have them to bring stones and build an altar of remembrance.

"These stones are to be a memorial to the people of Israel forever."   Joshua 4:7

Physical remembrances are important. An altar of remembrance, God said, for generations.

It is important to remember. Friends may not understand. They may look at your remembrances as a shrine and an indicator that you are not okay. However, this is not the case. Every parent has a refrigerator art display of their children's work or pictures. Yours is only slightly different. Every parent has a wall of portraits. Yours is equally valuable.

We find comfort in those things that hold our memories.

Suggestions of remembering include things such as:

JOURNALING.

Daily, or at least several times a week, write down your thoughts and feelings. Be honest. Go back in time and write of your anticipation, your devastation, and your present feelings.

Write a letter to your baby. Write the dreams you had planned and the love you experienced.

Write a letter to God. Share with Him all of your emotions.

PLANT A LIVING MEMORIAL.

Plant flowers, a bush, or tree at your home, or ask to have one planted in a park, a place where you may watch it grow as a reminder of your love.

CREATE A MEMORY AREA IN YOUR HOME.

This could be a photograph, a group of mementos that represent your baby. Or even special candles or a flower display. It is not a shrine but a memory of someone you loved. You could also choose a special object or piece of jewelry, something tangible to keep you connected and remind you of your baby.

Your memory becomes a treasure in your heart.

What are your stones of remembrance?

_____

_____

_____

Meagan and Mark's Story

I placed the fetal monitor on Meagan's abdomen and heard the steady beat of the fetal heart rate. At 138 it was a good rate with nice accelerations, indicating a happy, healthy baby.

Meagan and Mark, a very young couple, were happy and excited to be having their third baby. They had two little girls, Marisa and Melanie, three years and two years respectively, and now they were anxious to find out if this baby was a boy or girl. They enjoyed the anticipation and surprise and had elected to not find out ahead of time.

Meagan's labor had started spontaneously just five days ahead of her due date. As labor progressed quickly she asked for an epidural anesthesia and was soon comfortable. As the contractions became stronger we talked and laughed as they discussed possible names, all starting with an M, of course.

After only four short hours, Meagan delivered. "It's another girl!" shouted Mark as the doctor gently placed the slippery, wet baby onto the warmed blankets on Meagan's abdomen. Mark cut the cord, and they began to assist the nursery nurse in wiping the baby dry and stimulating her as she was not yet crying.

When she didn't respond to stimulation, we quickly transferred the baby girl to the resuscitation warmer to give her a little oxygen. I came around the room to assist the nursery nurse. As I placed the stethoscope on the baby's chest I observed that her little tummy was sunken, not the usual soft, round belly of a newborn.

Her heart rate was 110, a good rate, but still her skin tone was blue, and she was not responding to efforts to help her breath with the resuscitation bag and mask.

I pushed the emergency call for a code pink, alerting the baby code team.

We intubated and placed an ET tube to deliver oxygen directly into the bronchial tube. Squeezing the oxygen bag we didn't see the expected rise and fall of the chest from lungs filling with air. Her color was not improving. The door flew open as the Neonatal Intensive Care Unit (NICU) team began arriving.

Minutes seemed to click off in heartbeats, and she was now five minutes old. We reassessed the position of the ET tube, and I gave a quick report on the history of labor.

The baby was transported to the NICU, and I turned my attention to caring for Meagan and Mark, who were overwhelmed and distraught.

After taking care of Meagan's physical needs, I reviewed the recording of her labor. It had been textbook perfect. What had gone wrong?

I asked if I could pray with them and ask for God's presence with their little baby and comfort and strength for Meagan and Mark. Then I excused myself to the nursery so I could report back on what was progressing.

X-rays confirmed a diaphragmatic hernia, a condition in which the diaphragm develops a hole allowing the intestines to slip up into the chest cavity thereby preventing normal lung development.

It wasn't long before the neonatologist entered the room to explain the critical situation to Meagan and Mark. The baby was placed on a ventilator, but even that was not going to sustain the little one for long.

Meagan and Mark went to the nursery to keep vigil at her bedside. Family soon gathered in a family room. Little Marianne was removed from the ventilator and held lovingly by her parents with family present as she quietly passed.

Meagan and Mark kept her little body with them. They couldn't bear to let her go. When the funeral director arrived to take her little body, Mark carefully wrapped her in a soft blanket, carried her out of the birth place, and placed her in the car. It was the last loving act he could do for her. As the car pulled away, Mark crumpled on the ground and sobbed.

Six Years Later

While attending to my duties at work I was called to the front desk for a visitor. It was Meagan.

"I was in town and had to come by to see you," she said. "I wanted you to know how much it meant to us when you prayed with us at Marianne's birth°… and death. That whole experience changed our lives so much. We committed our lives to Christ and moved across the state, where Mark went to Bible College. He now pastors a little church in south Missouri. We are in town for a pastor's convention, and I couldn't leave without coming to see if you were still here."

Since moving away, they had another baby, a boy named Matthew. They had an empty place in their little family, but by treasuring the love and memories they found happiness, and joy had returned to their lives. They had been graced with the love and presence of little Marianne for only a short time, but their experience had transformed them and brought purpose and ministry into their lives.

> Praise be to the God and Father of our Lord Jesus Christ, the Father of compassion and the God of all comfort, who comforts us in all our troubles, so that we can comfort those in any trouble with the comfort we ourselves receive from God.
>
> —2 Corinthians 1:3-4

Stained Glass

Sun rising
Through stained glass
Shining
Beauty
The chapel of God
Pieces of your heart
Fragile, like glass
Broken
Shattered.
In the hands of the master craftsman.
He works His creative art
In patience
Mending
Healing
Fused by His touch
Son rising in your life
The light of life
Filters through
The stained-glass heart
Shining
Beauty
The chapel of God

Come to me, all you who are weary and burdened, and I will give you rest. Take my yoke upon you and learn from me, for I am gentle and humble in heart, and you will find rest for your souls.

—Matthew 11:28–29

There is no need to carry the burden of sorrow alone. God is there to help you. Be gentle with yourself. Do not put great expectations on how you think you should be acting or feeling. Allow yourself permission to mourn and cry. Everywhere around you will be reminders of what you have lost. When you least expect it, it will overpower you. You may want to alter plans or even traditions when necessary. You may not want to spend days with family or birthday celebrations, or baby showers for others. So, give yourself permission to decline. Don't offer your home for the holiday party if you are not up to it. Do not set yourself up for expectations from others. Express your feelings. You can decline graciously; "I don't think I am able to at this time." "I have been feeling a bit out of sorts and prefer to not attend." "I am sorry, but I can't do it this year." It's time to care for yourself.

Miracle in the Garden

At only twenty-six weeks Grace Maryalyce was born too soon. Her tiny body was whisked away to the NICU to competent care of nurses and doctors. The latest technology was used to supplant the womb that had, until now, sustained her life. And she lived. As the first critical hours passed she established her reputation as a fighter.

While Shawna recovered Joe went to the nursery to see his tiny daughter. She curled her little fist around his finger as if to say, "Hi, Daddy. I'm here." And with that she grabbed hold of his heartstrings forever.

The beeping, whirring, chirping sounds of the NICU became the familiar sounds of life for Shawna and Joe as they maintained vigil at the side of their firstborn. "Amazing" Grace they called her—God's little package of pure love. Where some couples falter under the stress, Shawna and Joe grew stronger, bonded together by their love for Grace.

As the weeks passed little Grace continued to amaze with her resilience to each challenge of survival. Then she developed pneumonia. The struggle for her premature lungs became too much, and after three months of life in the NICU, Grace Maryalyce died.

There are no words to describe the anguish in the heart of a parent, when dreams for the future and love for the life of a tiny child, is suddenly taken away.

I met Shawna and Joe when they came to the perinatal grief support group. Coming together helped them heal and work through the grief together. As they shared the story of their firstborn you could see, even through the tears, how she had blessed them with the love she had brought into their lives.

That spring the support group met together and made garden stepping stones, each decorated by the parents with smooth, colorful stones. Shawna and Joe carved, "Amazing Grace" across theirs and placed it in the Garden of Angels, St. Mary's infant memorial garden.

A year later, Shawna and Joe were anxiously anticipating the birth of another baby. Joe called to share the exciting news when she was safely delivered. Another little girl joined the family. She was full term and healthy. There were tears of joy ... and remembrance.

Later that same day I walked out to the garden. I couldn't believe what I saw. A yellow daffodil had pushed up through the ground *and* through the stepping stone, splitting it right between "Amazing" and "Grace." It was like a message from heaven that even through the trials of loss, love survives.

Shawna and Joe brought Miranda to see me. Together we walked out to the garden. There was the daffodil, still blooming right in the center of Amazing Grace. Today the stone is still there. They chose to not repair the crack but to leave it as a testament of love. Their miracle in the garden of God's Amazing Grace.

> God is our refuge and strength, an ever-present help in trouble. Therefore we will not fear, though the earth give way and the mountains fall into the heart of the sea, though its waters roar and foam and the mountains quake with their surging.
>
> —Psalm 46:1–3

> Hear, Lord, and be merciful to me; Lord be my help. You turned my wailing into dancing; you removed my sackcloth and clothed me with joy, that my heart may sing to you and not be silent. Lord my God, I will praise you forever.
>
> —Psalm 30:10–12

> Even though I walk through the darkest valley, I will fear no evil, for you are with me; your rod and your staff, they comfort me
>
> —Psalm 23:4

It is in the valleys of life that we find God's comforting presence. He is there to protect us and guide us. When we follow Him, He leads us to the higher ground. He is faithful and trustworthy.

When have you experienced God's presence in your valley?

_____

_____

_____

A Prayer of Blessing

If your grief is new, I pray for your peace and comfort in the days, weeks, months, and even years to come.

If you are plagued with painful memories, I pray for your reassurance of God's presence and grace.

If you are a mother whose arms and breasts are aching for the child you long to hold, I pray for healing peace and comfort.

If you are a father who is unable to cry, I pray for the flowing of healing tears and the capacity to express your grief.

If you are in deep depression, I pray for you to be lifted out of the valley.

If you are exhausted from grieving, I pray for you to be strengthened and refreshed to face another day.

For all of your needs, I pray that you will receive the understanding you need, and the assurance that you are loved, and that your mourning may turn to joy.

The world is full of suffering people. Those who survive are the ones willing to step forward into life and help others along the way.

You have been gifted with a special understanding for others suffering the loss of a precious baby and their hopes and dreams. You have a gift to share. Reach out, take the hand of God, regain your footing on a firm foundation, and then looking to Him, reach down and help lift another.

Grace and peace to you
from God our Father
and the Lord Jesus Christ.

Comfort
of
Heaven

He will wipe every tear from their eyes. There will be no more death, or mourning, or crying, or pain.

—Revelation 21:4

One of the promises to those who put their faith and trust in God is one of hope. The promise of eternal life—a new heaven and new earth.

Do Babies Go to Heaven?

You may ask that question. The Bible tells us yes, that indeed God's kingdom belongs to children.

Jesus said, "Let the little children come to me, and do not hinder them, for the kingdom of heaven belongs to such as these." Matthew 19:14

And he said: "I tell you the truth, unless you change and become like little children, you will never enter the kingdom of heaven. Matthew 18:3

If we hope to be reunited in heaven with our precious babies, we must become as little children in our hearts, completely trusting in our Father and wholly submitting ourselves to follow Him.

We have a beautiful picture of the hope of heaven in the story of King David recorded in the Bible.

The King's Mourning

David pleaded with God for the life of his baby boy. He fasted and spent the nights lying on the ground. The elders of his household stood beside him to get him up from the ground, but he refused, and he would not eat any food with them.

On the seventh day the child died. David's servants were afraid to tell him that the child was dead, for they thought, "While the child was still living, we spoke to David but he would not listen to us. How can we tell him the child is dead? He may do something desperate." David noticed that his servants were whispering among themselves and he realized the child was dead. "Is the child dead?" he asked. "Yes," they replied, "he is dead."

Then David got up from the ground. After he had washed, put on lotions and changed his clothes, he went into the house of the LORD and worshiped. Then he went to his own house, and at his request they served him food, and he ate. His servants asked him, "Why are you acting this way? While the child was alive, you fasted and wept, but now that the child is dead, you get up and eat!"

> While the child was still alive, I fasted and wept. I thought, 'Who knows? The Lord may be gracious to me and let the child live.' But now that he is dead, why should I fast? Can I bring him back again? I will go to him, but he will not return to me.
>
> —2 Samuel 12:22–23

David's hope was in the promise of eternity, to be reunited with his son in God's kingdom. He grieved, but he moved forward in life, fully trusting God for his future hope.

The promise of life eternal is given to all who put their faith and trust in God and seek the loving relationship God desires through Jesus Christ

> Surely your goodness and love will follow me all the days of my life, and I will dwell in the house of the Lord forever.
>
> —Psalm 23:6

When "the Lord is our Shepherd" and we follow Him in our life walk, then we have that same hope in heaven. We know that we will be reunited one day in God's kingdom. What a glorious day that will be!

> "What no eye has seen, what no ear has heard, and what no human mind has conceived" the things God has prepared for those who love him.
>
> —1 Corinthians 2:9

If you have been blessed by this little book, give thanks to God. He is the Comforter, the Counselor, the Father. He made the greatest sacrifice because of His love for you.

He understands your grief. He watched as His only Son was crucified at the hands of those He loved and came to save. But He is also the resurrection and the life! Jesus rose on the third day to give us hope—hope in a certain future with Him if we place our trust and our lives in His hands.

If you have not given your life to a relationship with Jesus, now is the best time. Ask Him into your life to forgive you, to comfort you, and to lead you. If you do this, then find a Bible-teaching church fellowship to become a part of.

May God bless each of you on your journey.

Helpful Resources for Baby Bereavement

Davis, Deborah L., PhD. Empty Cradle, Broken Heart. Golden Colorado: Fulcrum Publishing, 2016

Hinton, Clara. Silent Grief. Green forest AR: New Leaf Publishing group, 1998

Ilse, Sherokee, Empty Arms. Maple Plain, Minnesotta: Wintergreen Press, 1990

Guthrie, Nancy. Holding on to Hope. Carol Stream IL, Tyndale Momentum. 2002

www.mend.org: Mommies Enduring Neonatal Death
www.silentgrief.com: Hope for the grieving heart.
www.griefwatch.com: Resources for bereaved families and professional caregivers.
www.hannah.org: Christian-based support for infertility, pregnancy, or infant loss.
www.handonline.org: Helps families with miscarriage, stillbirth, infant death, and SIDS.
www.nationalshare.org: Pregnancy and infant loss support.

You can find the Wings of Hope community on Facebook.com.

Wings of Hope...

Because every life matters

About the Author

Shirley Bulen currently lives in Independence Missouri with her husband, a retired Air Force veteran. She has four children and is Nana to 12 grandchildren who are the light of her life. Her career spanned 45 years in Labor and Delivery and NICU, where she came close to parents whose babies died, as sometimes happens. Retired now, she is actively involved in her church and in her spare times she enjoys writing, painting, traveling and sharing the love of God.